If you don't have anything nice to say, don't say anything...

Or, say anything you like!

The Poison of Political Correctness

ISBN **978-1514166482**

Printed in the United States of America

The Poison of

POLITICAL
CORRECTNESS

By Lance Hodge

Introduction

*This book will be required reading for my EMT students, but it's more than that; it's essentially a discussion of kindness, empathy, and human decency. The meat of this book is a look into the nature of **Political Correctness** and a discussion of what it means to be a **Critical Thinker**, and my view of the insidious link between the two. As far as Critical Thinking goes, the insidiousness is in how Political Correctness has been able to capitalize on the lack of thinking, critically or otherwise.*

Although the focus here is initially aimed at my EMT students, this discussion is applicable for all; it's a discussion of our innate decent human nature, and how it is being perverted by the specter of Political Correctness run amuck. Whatever your thoughts about offensive speech, or Politically Correct speech, you should realize that 'free speech' is essential to a vibrant people imbued with a love of Freedom, and that free speech in the classroom is vital.

These are lessons for all, but hopefully this book will find its way into High Schools and into the hands of young people all over the country; it is our youth that is being poisoned and the cure is LIGHT. We must shine the light of truth and understanding, we must recognize lies and the nature of political agendas, if we are to save this Republic...

I'm a college professor. I teach an EMT (Emergency Medical Technician) course. I've been a licensed Paramedic for more than thirty-five years and worked for the *Los Angeles City Fire Department* for about twelve years before hurting my back carrying a man down some stairs. That call, and that injury, ultimately forced me to retire from the Fire Department and begin teaching students to become EMT's.

I was also a Los Angeles County Reserve Sheriff's Deputy for a few years, and I feel I have a well-rounded exposure to the various levels of society in a big city, including the underbelly, and the turmoil that exists among and between the races.

I take my job as a teacher seriously, and try to instill in my students the need for the highest level of *patient care* to *every* patient. Part of that discussion involves our prejudices. Most of us have some, we 'prejudge' people based on their physical appearance, the way they speak, their mannerisms, their clothing, their gender, all sorts of things, maybe even their color. I have always embraced that line from Martin Luther King, about judging a person not by the color of their skin but by the content of their character; I've always felt that way, even before Dr. King reminded us.

I talk to my students about such prejudices, and about tolerance, diversity, and patient care, and the need to remain sensitive to the differing cultures and beliefs we may encounter when treating our patients. It was one of those lectures, about the EMT's proper response to the behaviors or language or actions of our patients or of bystanders that ended up with me in Federal court defending my right to teach such a lesson.

Note: The *banned lecture* was essentially a lecture on *diversity* issues that I was 'ordered' to prepare for my students, after being reprimanded, and given a negative evaluation for "Lack of cultural sensitivity" for using the word "Witch Doctor" in class. That lecture, in which I used the hideous and hateful term *"Witch Doctor,"* was a lecture *discussing* diversity, tolerance, sensitivity to cultural issues, and the impact of Political Correctness. Then, after preparing that lecture, the college decided they didn't like it, and *banned* me from delivering it. That's the *short story* version.

This book begins with *that* lesson, the same lesson that ended up as evidence in court, with my college trying to assert their right to keep me from teaching it to my students, and to censor me from using certain words. No this wasn't in 1960, this was 2011. The Supreme Court had already made some significant rulings in this area but some aspects of free speech rights regarding college instructors were still somewhat unclear, at least to many college administrators around the country. But all this seemed crystal clear to *me*, and to my lawyer; those of us with common sense and a basic understanding of what our First Amendment means, and who understand the growing *sickness* that is Political Correctness.

But to these ardent supporters and enablers of the poison of Political Correctness, they were ready to charge ahead with guns blazing in order to keep me from speaking certain words, and from teaching my students this lesson. I was ordered not to teach the lesson and was not even allowed to hand it out to my students, under penalty of 'discipline' up to *termination*; the lesson was THAT terrible.

You're probably thinking, *"This guy has some sort of agenda, he's trying to push some wacky theories on these poor students."* You might think that there's more to this or the college wouldn't go through the trouble and spend all this money. Well, that lesson begins this book, *you* decide what sort of hidden agenda from some wacko college Professor is at work here. You decide.

After moving through the grievance process, and repeatedly appealing to the College President and even the Board of Trustees to see the obvious error of their ways, those college administrators, my Dean, their high-priced lawyers, and even the Board of Trustees, all figured they could convince a Federal judge to ignore several Supreme Court findings and suppress my right to free speech under the First Amendment of the United States Constitution, and they had LOTS of taxpayer money to waste to do it. So much for a financial crunch at our colleges.

Note to financial donors to Antelope Valley College in Lancaster, California: Where'd they get all this money to burn, did they spend any of YOUR donations on this court case? Of course not, not from donors, it was all tax-payer money, we can waste that money.

In a nutshell, the college wanted to keep me from saying the word "Witchdoctor" and of course "The N Word," or any *other* words

7

that anyone *might, perhaps,* in *some way, someday, maybe,* be *offended* by. I said, "No." My position was, I can teach these lessons to my EMT students about culture and words and offensiveness using whatever words I choose to use to teach that lesson, even that most hideous and offensive of words... *Witchdoctor.* (You can't make this stuff up.)

The college probably spent **more than a quarter of a million dollars** on this case. *They lost.* In the future it will be harder for some college to assert their right to censor an instructor, they'll have my case as a precedent and another example supporting the First Amendment.

As I mentioned earlier, this book will be required reading in my EMT class. They'll get the lesson that was banned as well as a short chapter at the end on *Critical Thinking,* since it is a lack of critical thinking, and a lack of fortitude for these many decades, that has allowed so many people, young and old, to simply *go along* with, and even champion, this PC agenda.

It's important that young people understand the *poison* of Political Correctness and how insidious this trend has become over the past many decades. This is a *little* book, about my little world, and how Political Correctness affected me and my ability to do my job, but it's a *big* message. There is much written on the subject and the examples could fill hundreds of pages, and has, and the scholarly work of others can demonstrate how the tentacles of the PC movement are intertwined throughout our daily lives, into the halls of our bureaucracies and institutions, and into the ether of our social networks. But the message isn't resonating, Political Correctness in all its forms is more pervasive now than ever. We see the effects recently as the label *racist* is used so freely that the meaning of the term has taken on some *other* definition, a nebulous one that seeks to paint all those who disagree, criticize, or comment, with the ugly color of a word intent on dividing us.

So here's the story of my little run-in with the machine of Political Correctness. You can judge for yourself how *dangerous* this lecture was, and why the college spent hundreds of thousands of dollars to try to stop it. I'm still perplexed by such stupidity, especially when it comes from those who hold the title "Educator."

Lance Hodge

Note: For those of you who have never been involved in a court case, there are some very annoying things, to say the least, that are allowed to occur. Each side 'states its case' and depositions are taken and people testify *under oath* to tell the truth. But, if one side tells lies, and there's no way to prove it, it's a 'he said, she said' situation, and those lies become part of the *record*. If you search *"Hodge vs. Antelope Valley College"* you'll get several reviews of this case from several sources, and in their effort to be fair, I guess, they take statements from both sides to write their articles. My College Dean, whose negative rating on my evaluation started all this, *(It was her offense to the word 'Witchdoctor' that prompted all this)* well she testified that I said certain cultural actions by patients or bystanders were "Weird," but I never said "Weird," not that that's a big deal, weird is weird, but I said "Unusual." Ok, not a BIG deal, but it grates on me that I'm being quoted as saying something I didn't say. *They* also say that I said "Witch stuff" when talking about unusual cultural practices the EMT might encounter, and I never said *that*. I don't even know what "Witch stuff" means; I'm a teacher, I'm usually pretty *literal*, and I wouldn't describe something as "Witch stuff" to my students because the first thing that would happen is someone would raise their hand and say, "What sort of witch stuff?" I think *the other side* said these things intentionally when reporters called in order to make this case more nebulous, or to paint me as some Wiccan with a *witch agenda*; they didn't want to see the headline *"Instructor banned from saying the word **Witch Doctor**."* This clarification probably didn't deserve a special note, but my Dean *lied* in her deposition about what I said and how I said it and those lies are now attributed to me, and I don't like that. I don't like liars.

Chapter One:

So, *this* happened...

THIS LESSON
IS <u>BANNED</u>

"I am directing you <u>NOT</u> to present the

Political Correctness vs.
The Real World lecture and
materials to the EMT 101 class"

**"FAILURE TO COMPLY WITH THIS
DIRECTIVE WILL SUBJECT YOU TO
DISCIPLINARY ACTION"**

Shane Turner, Assistant Superintendent/Vice President
Human Relations & Employee Relations, Antelope Valley College, November 23, 2010

TO: Antelope Valley College EMT students

FROM: Lance Hodge, Paramedic/EMT Instructor

SUBJECT: **"POLITICAL CORRECTNESS vs. THE REAL WORLD" LECTURE HANDOUT**

This lecture handout is/was banned. It was evaluated by college administration and they said, *"...the materials/lesson plans do not teach or address cultural diversity"* and they directed me *"... not to present the "Political Correctness vs. The Real Word" lecture and materials to the EMT 101 class."* They also noted, *"<u>Failure to comply with this directive will subject you to disciplinary action.</u>"*

That lecture must be <u>HORRIBLE</u>! Thank goodness we have college administrators to protect you children from evil speech! I imagine that reading a lecture like this could ruin you, make you CRAZY, cause riots, upset you, or even, OFFEND you, and could, heaven forbid, even make you start *discussing* various things and *thinking* all sorts of *THOUGHTS!* AAAAAHHHhhhhhh! RUN FOR YOUR LIVES, someone is trying to teach!

So you are either reading this letter alone, or college administration has changed its mind and the lecture is attached. Either way, I'm adding this letter and some notes:

The lecture you may or may not receive talked a lot about words, some *offensive* words, and the importance that EMT's respond appropriately when faced with difficult or surprising situations, such as offensive words or actions, or cultural actions or displays that the EMT might find unusual. A discussion of offensive words and dealing with unusual or unexpected situations isn't really complete without the discussion of several other related topics which are included in that lecture, things like; **cultural differences, political correctness, racism, prejudice, the *context* of words, free speech issues, The First Amendment, The Constitution, The Supreme Court, diversity, tolerance, race/religion/gender/body image, EMT safety issues, stereotypes, professionalism, 'alphabet words', ethics, morals, and more... whew.**

<u>Definitions of Cultural Diversity</u>: ethnic, gender, racial, and socioeconomic variety in a situation, institution, or group; the coexistence of different ethnic, gender, racial, and socioeconomic groups within one social unit...

Or, people of different origins, cultures and ways of life living alongside each other without one getting in the way of the other and trying to force their ways on other people...

Or, Cultural diversity is a peaceful coexistence of multiple cultures or societies in an organization (e.g. workplace or university.) A culture can be based on ethnicity (Hispanic, Asian), gender (male, female), age, sexual orientation or religion. Cultural diversity is also referred to as multiculturalism. Two of the key aspects of cultural diversity are coexistence without conflict and exchange of ideas.

Or perhaps, a variety or multiformity in race, ethnicity, language, tradition, culture, morality and religion existing within a community, organization, or population.

<u>And from the United Nations</u>: Everyone is entitled to human rights without discrimination of any kind. The non-discrimination principle is a fundamental rule of international law. This means that human rights are for all human beings, regardless of "race, color, sex, language, religion, political or other opinion, national or social origin, property, birth or other status." Non-discrimination protects individuals and groups against the denial and violation of their human rights. To deny human rights on the grounds of cultural distinction is discriminatory. Human rights are intended for everyone, in every culture.

We could discuss many *specific* cultural differences and list a hundred or a thousand cultural displays or rituals or things some people do that some people would find unusual, offensive, strange, shocking, or perhaps amusing, or we can accept some basic truths; the EMT will from time to time encounter situations during an emergency response that they find unusual, offensive, or sometimes shocking, and they must be respectful, understanding, and professional, and when possible allow the patient, family, or friends to engage in whatever cultural interactions that are important to them. In the lecture you may or not be allowed to receive I discuss a few specific incidents that I encountered as a Paramedic, and we will discuss possible appropriate as well as inappropriate responses to such situations that relate to the actions of EMS personnel.

Cultural diversity issues are essentially issues of tolerance, and for EMT's, *professionalism*. All of us realize we exist in a society of differences, with a multitude of intermixed cultures we co-exist peacefully and respectfully for the most part, and as EMT's we are dedicated to the promise that ALL people will be treated with the highest level of care and respect that we are capable of, as we would treat a loved one.

That lesson, of diversity, tolerance, and professionalism, is interspersed throughout the lecture on *"Political Correctness vs. The Real World."* Words, and things offensive, can play a huge role in issues of diversity and respect for others, and no lesson on cultural issues should stand alone. So here is the banned lecture, or not...

Lance Hodge, Paramedic/EMT Instructor

**BE CAREFUL,
WORDS ARE DANGEROUS,
WORDS CAUSE THOUGHT!**

DO NOT THINK!*

DANGER:
*MAKE SURE YOU *SPEAK* AND *HEAR* ONLY *APPROVED* WORDS!
*(The above warning has been a public service from your local college)

NOTE: The above letter did not have the lecture attached. That came later, after the lawsuit. **What follows is the banned lecture, unedited, in its entirety, too *horrible* for adult college students...**

Introduction/Summary of
"Political Correctness vs. The Real World" lecture

Lesson:

What is the appropriate EMT reaction to offensive language and actions or unusual cultural displays or behavior by patients or bystanders?

Background:

The EMT *will* be exposed to offensive or unusual behavior by patients and/or bystanders from time to time. Due to the effects of stress, illness or injury, medication or illegal drug effects, or cultural differences, such negative or unusual behavior will occur. The EMT must be able to appropriately deal with, and appropriately react to, rude, aggressive, strange, or offensive behavior during the course of their EMT duties. Keeping in mind that rapid and correct patient care is our mission, we must not allow outside influences to alter our calm, straight-thinking, professional, and focused delivery of medical treatment to our patients.

What is offensive?

There is *something* that would offend or shock each and every one of us. What is most important is how we *react* to such things or such *offense*. These things occur in everyday life and each of us reacts, some silently, some outwardly, some calmly, others with aggression. The way we choose to react to those things we are offended or surprised by may have significant and serious results. The scientific principle that "for every action there is an equal and opposite reaction" does not necessarily hold true to such human interaction. An offensive action may be VERY offensive, but our reaction to it need not be VERY significant. Another adage, "sticks and stones may break my bones, but words will never hurt me," needs to be looked at closely and understood for its wisdom. We began this paragraph with the question "What is offensive?" Most of us realize that what

17

is offensive to one person may not offend another. Most of us realize that a "word" has meaning based on the *context* of its use. We also know that cultural differences, sex, age, race, religion, and skin color, can make a word or action acceptable in one circumstance, and wholly *unacceptable* in another. With that in mind we enter the world of the "Politically correct" (PC). Most of us, understanding that words can hold great weight and the power to offend, think before we speak, altering what we say based on the audience around us and their likely reaction to certain words, we *self-censor*. This often occurs without much effort and has become second nature to most of us. Problems result when this self-censorship system breaks down, and a word or statement slips out that someone takes offense to, or for those who have no system of self-censorship and simply allow what they are thinking to go directly from the brain to the mouth. Not too long ago Don Imus, a talk radio personality, was fired from his radio job for using words that offended the black members of a girls' basketball team. These days the worst of the worst when it comes to offensive words are *racially* offensive words. As we said at the outset, *"There is <u>something</u> that would offend each and every one of us."* Balancing our First Amendment Constitutional right to Free Speech with our ability to survive in society, literally and financially, is the trick. Our free speech rights as decreed in the Constitution are one thing, they are about the *government* censoring you, but there are plenty of laws, rules, regulations, union agreements, *user* agreements, etc. that limit our freedom of speech. So we don't have a 'right' to say whatever we want, at least not without repercussions. That brings us back to being offended. If you say the wrong thing to the wrong person in the wrong way or in the wrong place, you might be in big trouble. It's safe to say that people are probably self-censoring more than ever, and that some words are on the verge of being effectively banned from our vocabulary, at least selectively.

Sticks and stones?

Nigger. THAT is one word that holds some weight, and is one of very few words whose mere utterance can instantly transform the speaker of it into a racist, can erase a career, and can lead to a cascade of negativity of Biblical proportions. I wonder if <u>that</u> *word* were erased, and replaced with, let's say, "The N-Word," if one day calling someone "The N-Word," as in "You N-Word!" if THAT would be banned, and we'd have to call it "The letter after M word." It's a *word*. It has some ugly history, to say the least, but it's a *word*, and saying it *doesn't* make you a racist; it's about *context*.

"**Racist person:** somebody who hates others who are not of his or her own race."

That's from the *Encarta* dictionary. I'm sure most dictionaries have a pretty similar definition, and that's the one I *thought* it was, so I'll go with that. Whew, I'm *not* a racist; I was worried for a second. I doubt that most of us, regardless of color, are. I'll bet that most of us, regardless of color, have some preconceived notions of others, even preconceived notions about others based on some particular color, or culture, or hair style, or car that they drive, or clothes they wear, or the food they like, or a myriad of other ideas that may or may not be correct based on some limited criteria we use to form these ideas.

"**Prejudice:** an opinion formed beforehand: a preformed opinion, usually an unfavorable one, based on insufficient knowledge, irrational feelings, or inaccurate stereotypes"

That's from Encarta too, and I'll bet most of us 'prejudge' people on some level or another, it's human nature, and in my opinion it's a GOOD thing. I'll get a little nervous if I'm on an airplane and five 'Arab looking' young men begin giving each other strange hand signals and begin to pray, fine, I'm prejudiced. *(Recently NPR reporter and commentator Juan Williams was fired for saying he gets nervous when he sees 'Muslim' looking men on an airplane)* Although we all do *some* prejudging of people, it could get you fired if you admit you do it!

It's safe to say that the word "racist" to describe people is tossed around *way* too much, and is mostly NOT accurate, even for someone who might use "The N-Word."

Context

Earlier I mentioned it's not so much the word but *how* you use it, the *context*. Context is everything! *"What's up Nigger, or Nigga?"* as a greeting vs. *"Get out of my way Nigger!"* The context is quite different, and therefore the *meaning* of the word is quite different. If I'm joking about basketball teams and I call a mostly black women's basketball team *'nappy-headed hos'* and I'm joking about black women's basketball teams, then I've used some slang and stereotypes as part of the banter, but to call that racism is, well, ridiculous. It may be *stupid*, but stupid isn't necessarily racism, stupid can simply be… stupid.

Here's what was said on a radio show between Don Imus and his producer Bernard McGuirk:

IMUS: *"That's some rough girls from Rutgers. Man, they got tattoos…"*
MCGUIRK (interrupting): *"Some hardcore ho's…"*
IMUS (picking up the 'ho' theme): *"That's some nappy-headed ho's there, I'm going to tell you that."* From Adversity.net

It's *context* that matters most, not words. When we start down the slippery slope of effectively banning certain words, we truly begin to dismantle the intent of the First Amendment of our Constitution. Our founding fathers and the Supreme Court have affirmed that as Americans the right of free speech is vital, even when the expression of that speech is repugnant to some.

20

The Offended

Since when did someone being "Offended" by something we say hold so much weight? In our effort to be *Politically Correct* and to please everyone, we have given 'The Offended' supreme power. Especially when a remark is racial or cultural in nature, however construed, the offended has met all the criteria needed to tar and feather them, oust them from their livelihood, and cast them from our midst. *"I was offended by that"* is the get out of jail free card, the Golden Ticket, and the only proof necessary to convict.

After the Imus controversy I was listening to a talk radio show, and a caller chimed in with this gem, that I think sums up the issue of offensive speech nicely.

(She was black, and I'm paraphrasing as best as I can remember her statement) *'Those Rutgers players should be ashamed of themselves. I teach my child that words have no power unless YOU give them power. Someone could call my child a nasty name and that won't make my child feel like less of a person, that word can't rob my child of their happiness, my child won't give that person the power to hurt them with a word.My child realizes that the word is more of a reflection of the character of the person using the word than it is a description of them. My child will not allow a word, any word, to have power over them.'*

I thought that was a great thing to teach a child, and something I taught my children. It's the old "Sticks and stones" but is still so true.

Don Imus didn't know those Rutgers basketball players. He didn't mean to actually imply that those girls were *whores*. He used *hos* as some borrowed cultural slang to mean they were rough girls, on the basketball court. Rough, basketball-playing girls, some with tattoos, and they were mostly black, hence *nappy-headed*. (Stevie Wonder in his song *I wish* sang, *"Looking back on when I was a little nappy headed boy"*) A quick Google search finds a wide array of businesses who use 'Nappy' in their title unapologetically, even celebratory, to sell their hair products and promote various hairstyles. Again, is it only blacks that can use *that* word too? Of course Don Imus was trying to paint those girls as some rough girls, and used various street slang to do it, but it was *banter*, maybe not well thought out, but banter, not the racist attack it was made out to be. *(For any of you who know about the charity work of Don Imus you know he doesn't hate black people.)* I mention the Imus incident because I'm a proponent of free speech; I believe that people should be able to express themselves without looking over their shoulder or worrying about losing their job, and I think the EMT student should have a good understanding of these issues to make sure that their speech is well thought out, and appropriate under the various circumstances they will encounter.

Don Imus used stereotypes as a general description of a tough basketball team. But, the fact that those comments 'offended' made the context of the remarks, or the comedy banter of that radio show, irrelevant. He lost his job.

Enter the EMT

With that background we can return to our point; the appropriate EMT reaction to offensive language and actions, or to things that shock or surprise the EMT while responding to an emergency situation. First, realize you have some baggage, we all do. The preceding several pages outlined just what you're up against. You've been raised in a PC environment most of your adult life, especially lately. You've been exposed to a barrage of media events where someone being offended by words was held out as the supreme arbiter of right and wrong, good and bad, and the judge of what constitutes racism or not.

But as an EMT responding to an emergency call you don't have the luxury of crying foul, calling the ACLU, or preparing evidence for a lawsuit because your patient or someone on scene calls you a name. Your job, your duty, is to deliver the best patient care possible, regardless of the person's race, sex, color, culture, religion, turban or cowboy hat, bald or hairy, skinny or fat, or talking nicely or calling you names. You don't have to *like* the patient, and you may not understand some of the things they do or say when it comes to their particular upbringing or culture, but you should give them the sort of care you would give to your mother or father, wife or husband, son or daughter, etc. So, in our job, if the patient calls you a *Nigger* (especially if you're black) you'll let that slide, you'll continue to be a calm and professional EMT, and you'll attempt to give that patient the best care you know how to deliver. "Sticks and stones..."

Summary

You may agree that certain words should never be spoken, regardless of the reason, but one thing is certain, as an EMT such words you encounter WILL be the <u>actual</u> **WORDS**, not some alphabet code for the words. And just as some students in my classes gasp when they hear such words, or file official complaints, or drop the class, we must all be *aware* of our reaction to such words, and most importantly we must insure that our patient care isn't negatively impacted when we find ourselves offended during an emergency response.

All our patients deserve our best care. All patients should be treated rapidly, appropriately, and with compassion. Of course we will do our best to be sensitive to other cultures and beliefs, and to never use words that might offend while working as an EMT, but our *patients* may use offensive words, and they may do things that shock or surprise us, and we must remain professional and deliver proper patient care even if someone on the scene of an emergency pushes our buttons or offends or surprises our sensibilities.

Moral of the story

"Sticks and stones may break my bones, but words will never hurt me." YOU give words power, or make them powerless, it's up to you.

Antelope Valley College

EMT101

<u>Political Correctness vs. The Real World</u>:

The EMT and professionalism in the face of offensive or surprising language or behavior, and our understanding of diversity, stereotyping, prejudice, and cultural differences.

By Lance Hodge, Paramedic
EMT Instructor

This lesson focuses on two main topics; the need for EMT students to participate in a frank, free, and open discussion of offensive language and behavior or strange or surprising actions that they may encounter, along with its relationship to stereotyping, prejudice, racism, cultural differences, and professionalism, and the effect of political correctness on this discussion in the college setting.

<u>NOTICE</u>: *This lecture material is intended for adults. EMT students in this class must be at least 18 years old.*

<u>Introduction:</u>

Shit. I mean, "Darn it." Crude language can get you into trouble. The world is becoming increasingly PC (Politically Correct) and the *offended* are being given greater and greater weight in today's society. Some of you may yourselves use 'swear words,' some quite freely, and some of you may find even the tamest of 'dirty words' quite offensive. **Diversity**; we are different. We all have somewhat different upbringings, cultural differences, beliefs and sensitivities; and we should remember that *diversity* and *tolerance* is about understanding those differences, and treating each other with appropriate respect and dignity, which goes both ways, in that we must learn to accept our differences rather than try to make others conform to *our* beliefs. THAT is diversity and tolerance. We should realize that there will always be *someone* offended by *something*, and that that is OK; we'll never be able to insure that "offense" never occurs; we must learn to accept differences and to deal with others, even when we sometimes find the actions or words of others distasteful. Although our freedom of speech is not without limits, our founding fathers and numerous court decisions since have put great weight in allowing each of us free expression of our views, even when some consider that speech *vile*. It is such vile or offensive speech that is most in need of protection to ensure that we as a society feel free to express our views, whatever they may be. "Political Correctness" continues to erode such protections, leading us ever closer to some Orwellian future where the speech police tell you what words you may or may not speak.

The EMT will find themselves working in an environment where people of virtually every conceivable culture, race, color, background, upbringing, and sensitivity will be part of their emergency response sooner or later. We live in a world were diversity is the norm, and differences between us can sometimes be profound.

What offends one person may not offend another. A word that is acceptable in one situation may be wholly out of place in another. A friendly greeting to one person can be the worst imaginable insult to another. To put it mildly, we need to choose our words carefully, and, perhaps unfortunately, we need to alter our speech based on the sex, race, color, and the culture of those around us.
This lecture is intended to get you thinking, *intensively* and *critically*.

"The function of education is to teach one to think intensively and to think critically. Intelligence plus character – that is the goal of true education" *

As EMTs we will work closely with Nurses, Doctors, Paramedics, Police, and Firefighters, and will interact constantly with the wide array of diverse people in our community. We will encounter people who are angry, stressed, intoxicated, rude, and even violent. Our first instinct is to rightly conclude that their medical condition and/or events surrounding the incident has brought them to this point and has *caused* this behavior. With professionalism and understanding we can look beyond their bad behavior and deliver to them the highest level of care we can give. Our patients will sometimes push our limits, using profanity or personal insults that may trigger deep-seated anger and resentment toward your patient or others. You might work for years and never encounter offensive language, or it might occur on your first call as an EMT, we never know.

As emergency responders we must remain calm, straight thinking, caring, and focused. We must deliver to EVERY patient the highest level of care, <u>as if we were treating a loved one</u>.

What words are 'trigger words' for you? Words that could cause you to react in kind to your patient, words that could cloud your judgment, words that might cause you to lose your focus on patient care and in some cases to verbally or even physically assault your patient. Are there such words, in the right context, and in the right situation, that could do that to you?

If the answer to the above was no, that's great. It sounds like you can stay focused on the task of quick and appropriate patient care regardless of verbal provocation. If you answered yes, then... *"Houston, we have a problem."*

Nigger. Kike. Cunt. Fatty...

Ouch, words can hurt. Race, religion, sex, body image are some potential triggers and possible hot buttons that could be pushed by patients, family, or bystanders during an emergency response. If you find yourself taken aback reading such words, or hearing such words, you might be susceptible to reacting in an inappropriate manner if such trigger words were used toward you at the scene of an emergency. Realizing that you are *sensitive* to certain words is the first step in controlling your response to them.

"Let no man pull you low enough to hate him" *

Again, as EMTs we should assume that a rude or verbally combative patient is suffering from a medical condition and is in need of our help. Of course we always have the option of awaiting the arrival of the police if our *safety* is at risk. We can even *leave* the scene until the police have arrived and have made sure it is safe. When it comes to offensive words or behavior, we must be able to concentrate on patient care, and not on dirty words or rude actions, but not at the risk of our safety.

* The quotations on this and the previous page were from Dr. Martin Luther King Jr.

The EMT: A unique role

The EMT faces situations that few professions encounter. EMTs work in every imaginable social environment from the poorest to the wealthiest neighborhoods, with the young and the old, and with the most respectful and well-behaved and the most disrespectful and unruly. As medical professionals in such diverse environments we must be ever aware of the potential dangers around us and realize that our safety comes *first*, even in the face of someone in distress whose very life may hang in the balance.

This lesson is essentially a lesson on *safety*, but comes from the dangers within *us,* that may impact not only ourselves but also the well-being of our patients. All of us have some stereotypical ideas. We prejudge others and situations every day, most often instinctually. We judge others based on their appearance, their voice, their demeanor, etc. We stereotype people, and it's a natural, normal, and *valuable* human mechanism; like anything, we can of course use stereotyping wrongly, to unfairly judge people, and as a tool to serve an irrational prejudice.

Stereotype: *an oversimplified standardized image of a person or group*

Prejudice: *a preformed/preconceived judgment or opinion, usually an unfavorable one, based on insufficient knowledge, irrational feelings, or inaccurate stereotypes*

If someone is running down the street screaming while waving a pistol in the air and shooting, we are wise to get out of the way, to seek cover, to hide, or to run away, because this person *seems* to present a danger to us. We have made a quick judgment; we have stereotyped this person, perhaps as a *crazy killer.* It's possible that this person is not a danger to us at all, that they may even need our help. If we found out more about the situation we might make a different choice about what to do; but we *needed* to make a quick decision, we *needed* to stereotype this person; it is a survival mechanism, and in this case it's a *good* thing.

Race, religion, gender, general appearance. These are perhaps the top four areas in which most of us use stereotyping of people, and perhaps have prejudices. Most of us want to treat others with dignity and respect. Most of us are not evil. Most of us are not racists. Most of us try to treat others as we would like to be treated. Most of us are good people. Those are some very general statements, but I think they are generally true.

Racist: *prejudiced against all people who belong to other races*

Prejudice and Stereotyping:

It's 2 a.m.; it's a bad part of town. You are walking alone. You are about to cross the street when you notice a group of five young men walking toward you on the other side of the street. The way they are dressed makes you think they may be in a gang. Do you cross the street now or wait until they have passed to cross?

You've made some judgments here. You had previously decided this was a bad part of town. You have now decided these young men might be gang members, and now you are about to decide if it is wise to place yourself in close proximity to these young men that you have judged to be a potential threat to you.

You think about racism, prejudice, and stereotyping and decide to cross the street as you had intended to do in the first place, after all you don't know anything about these young men, and they might be wonderful people. As you pass the young men they stop and ask you for five dollars, you say you don't have five dollars, or you give them five dollars, regardless of your choice they grab you, hit you in the face, throw you to the ground, kick you in the head until you are unconscious, then they go through your pockets, take your wallet, your cell phone, and your keys, kick you in the head again, and continue on their way. You die later of your injuries.

Or, you decide to stay on your side of the street until the young men pass, but *they* cross the street and the above situation occurs anyway.

Or, you cross the street, you pass the young men who say "How ya doin" you say "Good" and nothing happens.

Or, you stay on your side of the street, the young men go by on the other side, and nothing happens.

Do you think ALL these, or other scenarios are possible? Of course they are, but what would happen if YOU faced that situation, which might occur? Who knows, we *never* KNOW, we make judgments and we take actions based on a whole range of factors, including our past experiences and/or our stereotypes and prejudices.

What's the point? We make choices, we size up situations, we PREJUDGE, we use stereotypes, and for the most part we do this as a survival mechanism. It turns out that FBI statistics DO show that this was a bad part of town; you already believed that based on your experiences and the experiences of your friends and crime reports on the local news. You took the data available to you and prejudged or *stereotyped* this part of town, you were right. It turns out that those five young men WERE gang members, were wearing gang attire, and were going to assault and rob anyone they found that seemed vulnerable. You didn't KNOW that, but it may have been *reasonable* to assume it, for safety sake.

Had you given more thought about your night on the town maybe you wouldn't have stayed out so late, maybe you would have chosen a different part of town, maybe you would have parked closer. Maybe stereotypes, prejudice (prejudging) and good judgment would have kept you alive that night. My point is that it's OK to judge people and situations without ALL the information, since it is rarely possible to have ALL the information in most cases. Although "prejudice" has come to mean something negative, or to have *racial* implications, *prejudice* at its core is not necessarily a negative, it is simply to 'prejudge.' We all have prejudices, we all prejudge, sometimes fairly, sometimes not. As the above example might show, it can be a *good* thing.

As a paramedic, and in my personal life, I have encountered several situations that illustrate stereotypes, prejudice, and good and bad judgment. I once owned a house that needed a new roof. I had two 'contractors' come over and give me estimates on the job. The first showed up in a nice new truck with his company logo and information painted on the side, he was well-groomed and well-dressed and very professional. His estimate seemed too expensive. The second roofer showed up in an old beat up truck, he was dressed in dirty jeans, and he had long hair and lots of tattoos. His estimate was *much* lower. I thought for a moment about the two men, and about my own stereotypes of people, and decided to give the job to the dirty longhaired tattooed man. A few months later when it rained, the roof leaked. After trying to get hold of the man again I found out he wasn't actually a licensed contractor as he said he was, and I wished I had trusted my instincts. I wished I had trusted my stereotyping of that man and *had* been prejudiced against him based on the things I observed and felt. In this case, giving him the benefit of the doubt ended up costing me a lot of money.

When it comes to stereotyping and prejudice, I hope you do, and I hope you are. *(Which means you allow yourself to trust your instincts and intuition, and you incorporate things you know and/or believe into your decision-making. **Prejudging** is part of learning, we often make decisions with incomplete information; we usually don't have ALL the information)* Your moral and ethical values and upbringing should allow you to discard obviously flawed thinking related to untrue or unrealistic stereotypes, and or harmful prejudices, while allowing you to make educated 'judgments.'

True story: One night at a fire station in Watts, two young teenage girls rang the doorbell at 1 a.m. They needed directions to a nearby street where they had parked their car; we explained that this was a bad part of town with frequent murders and rapes in the area, and that we would call the police who could escort them to their car. They refused, saying, *"If you don't do anything to people, they won't do anything to you"* and they left. As they walked away, I reminded them again of the danger. No, we didn't get a call later to them raped and murdered, but it wouldn't have surprised me at all. You might think their action was proper, thinking the best of people, not stereotyping this neighborhood or its people and showing no prejudice (prejudgment) even when faced with the FACTS we related to them that there <u>was</u> danger in walking at night in this neighborhood. You might admire their choice, and their judgment, I found it STUPID.

OK, we generally **do** stereotype people and situations. We generally **do** have prejudices or preconceived notions based on incomplete data about various things and people. Generally, and to varying degrees, we ALL do this. Although some of you, and those girls above, may be so *evolved* that you operate on a much higher plane than we other mere mortals. It is important to know that we do these things, often without thinking much about it. People develop terms such as "inherent" or "unconscious bias" and other psychobabble to paint our common sense and judgment as something negative, or as racism. Such awareness may help us make sure that our stereotyping and prejudices are grounded in some reality, and that we work to discard those stereotypes and prejudices that are simply wrong, hurtful, dangerous, or destructive. But we should accept the fact that we all *judge*, and it's often a positive not a negative.

When I speak here of the value of stereotyping and prejudging, I am really talking about using *good judgment*.

The title of this lesson speaks of political correctness, professionalism, offensive language and behavior, and of understanding stereotyping and prejudice. It is the current state of *political correctness* that makes this lesson vital. Too often, because of political correctness, we don't talk frankly about matters of sex, race, or religion, because of the risk of offending someone.

Political correctness: *relating to or supporting the use of language or conduct that deliberately avoids giving offense, e.g. on the basis of ethnic origin or sexual orientation or conforming to a belief that language and practices which could offend political sensibilities (as in matters of sex or race) should be eliminated*

If we are to conform to the previously stated *standard* then we must not speak of anything that COULD, potentially, offend someone's sensibilities. We are arriving at a place where we are not **allowed** to hurt someone's feelings.

"Language and practices which could offend political sensibilities should be eliminated."

So political correctness is really about outlawing certain words or things one does that 'could' offend; banning words, outlawing certain speech, banning certain 'jokes,' because someone *might* be offended. Such outlawed speech takes us down a dangerous road and impacts the most essential aspect of our freedom as Americans; our right to speak freely and openly. Of course these 'freedoms' are possessed in the face of common sense, appropriateness, and good judgment. Certainly, we all edit ourselves in some situations; perhaps at work, in certain surroundings, or depending on the people present. Here, as EMT students, the frank discussion of these topics is vital to the *safety* of the EMT and their patients. We should be able to hear and to discuss offensive words as part of this lesson.

Offensive words: *nigger*

That word more than any other in American society is the poster child of a non-politically correct word. We could substitute other offensive words for the sake of this lesson, but *that* word illustrates the point as perhaps no other word could. It wasn't that long ago that comedians would use that word as a main part of their stand-up comedy (Chris Rock as one example.) I imagine Chris Rock still gets away with it, but some comedy clubs have banned that word and will not allow a comedian (black or white) to perform at the club again if that word is used. Chris Rock is black. There is a BIG difference in 'who' uses this word as to the offense it might cause, and certainly there is a HUGE factor in *how* the word is used. There certainly was a time, recently, when the *context* of using that word mattered, but now the word itself has become such a pariah that context no longer seems to matter. There are *colleges* where professors who *speak* that word in a lesson have been fired, and others that have been threatened with losing their job, even when the lesson is *about* the word, even when the lesson is a lesson on understanding the offensive nature of words and an EMT's response to them!

WORDS:

We know words are powerful. We know words can hurt. We know that our right to "Free speech" has limitations, *(We are not free to shout "FIRE" in a crowded theater if there is no fire, at least not without possible repercussions.)* Political correctness has evolved to the point where we may need instruction on banned words so as not to get fired from our jobs or, one day, be locked up in jail for speaking them.

Depending on **how** you say it, **when** you say it, **where** you say it, or *why* you say it, the following words could get you in big trouble:

How many offensive alphabet words do you know?

The "A" word

The "B" word

The "C" word

The "D" word

The "E" word

The "F" word

The "G" word

The "H" word

The "I" word

The "J" word

The "K" word

The "L" word

The "M" word

The "N" word

The "O" word

The "P" word

The "Q" word

The "R" word

The "S" word

The "T" word

The "U" word

The "V" word

The "W" word

The "X" word

The "Y" word

The "Z" word

As EMTs we must me mindful of our words. We are medical professionals, and we often deal with people who are sick, stressed, angry, sad, unbalanced, suicidal, homicidal, etc., and the words we use, and how we use them, can help people calm down, feel safe, and can even defuse a dangerous situation. Our words can also set someone off and escalate a situation into one that could get *us* hurt or killed. And, of course, the use of the wrong 'alphabet' word could *offend*, and even get us fired.

As professional EMTs we are responsible for upholding the good reputation that has been earned by thousands of EMTs before us. The public generally respects our profession and expects the highest standards from us. Our ethical and moral standards must be high, and we should take pride in maintaining the public's trust in us. Part of this high standard involves language. Our patients may curse, we should not. Our patients may say or do things offensive to us, but we should respond calmly and professionally.

I worked as a Paramedic with the Los Angeles City Fire Department for 13 years, responding to more than 15,000 9-1-1 calls during my career. The following situation occurred to me while working in Pacoima, CA at Fire Station 98. I was, and am, white, my partner was Hispanic, and the four fire fighters on Engine Company 98 that responded with us that day were black.

The call was for a possible heart attack. We arrived a few minutes before the engine company. The house was 'decorated' with dozens of bumper stickers with anti-black sayings, and a large confederate flag hung outside. Using my skills at stereotyping, I concluded we were entering the house of a racist, who hated black people.

The man on the couch was conscious, and after a brief exam and a look at his EKG we concluded he was likely having a myocardial infarction (Heart Attack) and we began to explain what we were going to do (IV, medication, transport to the hospital). The man was sweating profusely but was alert and cooperative.

The Engine Company pulled up outside and a moment later the Captain, followed by two firemen, entered the man's house. Immediately the man said to me, "*Get those niggers out of my house.*" He seemed very upset. I explained that they were the EMT firefighters and they needed to help us set up the IV and move the gurney. The man became more upset and said, "*I want those mother-fucking niggers out of my fucking house.*" He repeated 'fucking' 'mother-fucking' and 'niggers' several more times until we were quite sure of the point he was trying to make, and realized he probably wasn't raised in a PC household. The Captain, who had been silent, said to me, "*We'll be right outside if you need us*" and they left the room. I tried to explain again to the man that they were here to help him, and he replied by saying, "*Keep those fucking niggers away from me.*" We proceeded to start the IV, contact the hospital, and give the man medication. When we had the man on the gurney, I went out first and told the Captain we could handle it, and the Engine Company left. We transported the man to the hospital.

So, was that OK?

Should I have said something different?

Should the black Captain have said something to the man?

Should the firefighters have done something other than what they did?

What would YOU have done if you were me, or if you were the black firefighters?

And, if you would have handled this call differently, what are the negative and/or positive possibilities of your actions?

NOTE: Be prepared to discuss the above scenario and your ideas of the proper response for EMTs encountering such behavior.

Throughout this lesson you could, and **should**, substitute *other* offensive words for "The N word." The "N" word is just an example to illustrate the point, you should be aware of words that might offend YOU. It's important to know if **you** have words or actions that 'push your buttons.' Some people know there are words that could provoke them, and some people could be *so* provoked as to hit somebody (generally a BAD idea.) Some people would even *shoot or stab* a person for using a certain word toward them. There are all sorts of people, and they react in all sorts of ways, to all sorts of things, sometimes in ways we can't understand or even conceive of, and sometimes to things *we* think are *trivial*. We all have sensibilities, we can all have our feelings hurt, and as an EMT you MUST be aware of potential triggers that could upset you and you MUST be able to deal with such insults and the anger it could provoke, in a calm and professional manner. If you don't think of such things *before* they happen, you could find yourself acting instinctively, and perhaps inappropriately to offensive words. You might work your entire EMS career and never encounter offensive language used in your presence, or it could happen on your first call; we need to be prepared to react calmly, professionally, and appropriately should this occur. If words or examples are used in this class that make you uncomfortable they may be there for a reason, and a *lesson*. As EMTs we cannot be so sensitive to 'words' that they negatively affect our judgment, we must allow them to pass over us harmlessly and continue doing our job.

One reason a lesson such as this 'should' be **spoken**, rather than simply read, is to *hear* these words out loud. *(I realize that many of you are no strangers to bad words, some of you probably talk like drunken sailors with your friends and hearing a nasty word in this class is nothing special. But there are many people who don't use that language and are easily offended by it, and who must, as an EMT, learn to deal with exposure to such language, and who must, to a large degree, become desensitized to such offensive words and actions.)* There is little shock value in someone saying, or you reading, "N word," or me saying you must be aware that "pejoratives" may be used in the field. But there can be a substantial and visceral reaction to *hearing* the word "Nigger" spoken. I have heard students gasp when the word nigger was used in class, and I have had black EMT students become so upset at hearing the word, even as part of a story and a lesson, that they filed a formal complaint. Think of that for a moment, an *EMT* student so upset at simply *hearing* the word nigger, used in a college classroom, in a story about a racist who uses that word, that they would complain about the instructor for simply *speaking* the word in that lesson! What would this person do if they were an EMT, and during a medical call some racist patient *called them a nigger?* I can envision that student responding inappropriately. Any of you who find yourself offended by this lesson, or the words in it, have just learned something valuable, you have a sensitivity that you must understand and be able to control if you are to work as an EMT.

In Chicago several years ago, a 9-1-1 dispatcher received a call for help. Someone had been shot and was bleeding on the front lawn. *(This isn't the exact conversation but is similar.)* While the dispatcher was gathering information from the caller the caller said something to the effect, *"Quit*

asking fucking questions and get an ambulance out here."
The dispatcher told the man not to use that language. The
man said, *"What the fuck, this guy's dying."* The dispatcher
warned the man again about his language and said she
would hang up if he used curse words again; he said, "*This
guy's fucking dying..."* and she hung up. He called back,
cursed again, and she hung up again. An ambulance was
finally dispatched to the call, but it was delayed by the
dispatcher's actions. The man died. The dispatcher was
fired. Most of us see that this dispatcher should not have
responded to the dirty words, she should have simply
gathered the information she needed, given instructions to
the man, and dispatched the proper resources to the call.
She allowed herself, and her duty as a dispatcher, to be
adversely affected by curse words that offended her. *That* is
a perfect example of why this lesson is so important.

Professionalism: *the skill, competence, or character expected of a*
member of a highly trained profession

We are professionals. We are expected to possess a high
level of skill as an EMT. We are expected to be competent in
what we have been trained to do, and we should
demonstrate a character based on high ethical and moral
standards. Taking into consideration the diversity of our
patients, bystanders, and those with whom we work, we
should be considerate in our language and actions. We
understand that race, gender, religion, and culture are
variables that might be difficult to fully understand or
identify with, and that what we do and say, and *how* we do
or say things, can have a profound impact upon people. It's
one thing to discuss these issues here, and speak these
words here, in a learning environment, as opposed to casual
use on your job, or with the general public, or your patients,
and we need to appreciate that difference.

On the topic of cultural differences and beliefs, I once told a story in class of a patient whose family was chanting over him and waving an object that looked like a 'witch doctor' would use, and I raised my arm and shook my head the way the man had during that ceremony, and someone in class laughed at my demonstration. The Dean of the Department was in my class that day evaluating me. That story, the word 'witch doctor,' and my demonstration of what that ceremony looked like, was included in my evaluation as a negative rating, as something I shouldn't have said and done, because it *could* offend someone, and because it caused someone in the class to laugh. I probably should show up in class and say, *"Let's turn to page 117"* and start reading; perhaps that's what teaching is coming to. But these lessons are important; years of experience make an instructor's lessons a valuable insight and should be shared as a way to illustrate the lesson. Political correctness can have a very negative and chilling effect on what information an instructor feels comfortable sharing with their students, and editing out some stories could result in a future safety risk to the EMT student. One day, as an experienced EMT, you may find yourself training a new EMT on the job. YOU might find yourself discussing a topic like this, YOU may become the teacher, and hopefully you will feel able to discuss such topics freely. Just so you know, after that discussion of unusual cultural beliefs, not one witch doctor in the class complained about that story.

If 'dirty words,' or a story relating a stereotype points out a relevant lesson, or makes a point that needs to be made, then in this classroom that story may be told and those words used; certainly there is a time and a place for such language, especially in a germane discussion as part of a lesson about such words! As an EMT foul language should generally be left at home, unless you have kids! We are held to a high standard of professionalism by our patients and the public we encounter, and we should live up to that expectation. This lesson hinges on common sense, good judgment, and personal character, along with the ability to 'tolerate' offensive language or behavior in order to deliver the highest level of care to <u>every</u> patient.

Tolerance: the attitude of someone who is willing to accept someone else's beliefs, way of life, etc., without criticizing them, even if they disagree with them; the ability to experience something unpleasant or painful without being harmed

<u>Summary</u>:

Tolerance is not a one-way street. Free speech *can* be restricted when such speech presents a clear danger, but it is *offensive* speech, the kind we are discussing here, that needs protection, and it was just such offensive speech the 1st Amendment sought to safeguard. Any of us could do or say something that hurts someone's feelings, or that offends them, and we might have no intention of doing so, and, whether we intend to use speech to offend or not, it is this free expression that should, in most cases, be vigorously defended. Isn't 'tolerance' **the ability to experience something unpleasant or painful without being harmed** (as in *tolerating* the vulgar or otherwise offensive language of your patient, or even that of a college professor?) As professional EMTs we will properly edit ourselves on the job and remain professional in our responses to bad behavior; while our patients may freely and vigorously demonstrate <u>their</u> freedom of expression!

Perhaps tolerance is in realizing when words are simply words, not swords. The old saying, *"Sticks and stones can break my bones, but words can never hurt me"* should be embraced. It is *we* who *allow* words to become swords. They are only words. One positive outcome from offensive language when used on us as a tool to hurt, is that those words are a window into the person *speaking them*, those words often illustrate the ignorance of the one using them, and **do not** define the person that the word is used against.

Words have no power on their own, you must *give* them power; you must *allow* them to hurt.

The example I used earlier, of *saying* "The N word," it is clear that that word could hurt, just hearing it. But there is a lesson in hearing that word and others like it; we must be able to understand where political correctness is carried too far, sometimes we must be able to discuss matters that are uncomfortable, to learn. I believe we must not arrive at a place in society where certain words are banned. Given a choice, I would rather see words thrown than stones. Words are tools to express ourselves, the good and the bad, and to allow us to learn and to grow.

Character: *the aggregate of features and traits that form the individual nature of the person, such as moral qualities, ethical standards, principles, honesty, integrity, courage, and reputation*

Perhaps there will be a time when we as a society are all colorblind, when the content of our character is what matters. A good start is to embrace that in your own life, *to judge people by their **character***, to let go of inaccurate prejudices and stereotypes, and to let character define us all.

P.S.
The previous story of the Pacoima racist was often used as an example in my EMT classes. The story is true. The things quoted are what the patient actually said, although I believe the tone, volume, and body language of the patient made the impact of those words 100 times more intense than the way I deliver it to my classes. Regarding the upward spiraling politically correct nature of the world, it may or may not

surprise you to know that simply telling that story, to adults, in my EMT class, as a lesson on how to respond to offensive language and behavior, resulted in a complaint against me, a tenured college professor, Paramedic, EMT Instructor, because two students were 'offended' by hearing the word 'nigger' during that lesson. They thought I didn't need to use that word, and at least one of them dropped the EMT course after that class. Of course, since the word was used in the context of teaching a college lesson about offensive language, and was germane to that topic, the college responded by telling those students they should have listened to the lesson being taught; and that their overreaction to hearing that word is exactly the sort of thing they must NOT do as an EMT.... Ah, that's what I <u>hoped</u> the college would say, but instead, they threatened to fire me because of that complaint. Wow. The Politically Correct freight train is chugging along, and some of us are being thrown under the wheels.

That racist in Pacoima, if he had gone into cardiac arrest, you know that those black firemen would have rushed back in to perform CPR on him, and they would have done it to the best of their ability. They would have treated that man as if he were someone they knew and cared for, even though they knew <u>what</u> he was, and they knew what **he** thought of them. They would have tried their best to save his life, that's what we do, **that** is a reflection of **our** character.

L.Hodge/EMT101

     That was it. The *hideous* lesson that just shouldn't be taught.

Postscript:
You were able to read this lecture, and discuss this subject in class, because a Federal Court Judge ruled that this subject is a matter of *public concern*, is relevant to the training of EMTs, and is protected speech under the First Amendment of the United States Constitution. **It took *that*, four years and a lawsuit against *Antelope Valley College*, to be able to give you this material and to discuss it openly in our classroom; you should find that shocking.**

This lecture discussed *Political Correctness*; it is out of control Political Correctness which prompted this college to find my use of the word "Witch doctor" so potentially offensive, to some unknown person, some day, maybe, to give me a negative evaluation for using it, and to tell me not to say it again, and to be willing to go to Federal Court and spend a quarter of a million dollars or more of taxpayer's money to suppress the ability to teach this lesson. Wow. *Witch doctor*. So keep this lesson in mind when working as an EMT. Your employer WILL have restrictions on your speech, which is generally allowable, but you must be cautious about the aspects of Political Correctness in today's society, and in your workplace, who knows what *your* employer might find potentially offensive. As EMTs we should strive to be professional and respectful at all times, even when our patients or bystanders are not.

A <u>classroom</u> is *supposed* to be a place where ideas can be discussed, even *controversial* or **offensive** ideas or language, but the work environment *is different*, and rightly so. Your employer seeks to maintain a business that serves the public, one without controversy, and so might be quite sensitive to the concept of being *Politically Correct*. As EMTs we are sensitive to that, professional, and will always treat our patients with respect and dignity, and whenever possible to be willing to allow their expression of personal or cultural beliefs; that respect for the diversity of our human community is a core concept for all people, and especially for we in the EMS community.

If you'd like an example of Political Correctness infecting an institution, you can find one at *Antelope Valley College* in Lancaster, California.

*Note to donors, **they** seem to have plenty of money to waste, maybe there's a nice charity that needs your help instead?*

P.S. The Dean, the college President, the head of Human Resources, The Board of Trustees, etc., none of them apologized for what they'd done. None showed regret or acknowledged they were in error. As far as I can tell they still think they were right. They still embrace the poison of Political Correctness, and they aren't alone. You probably have a college next door to you filled with similar people thinking similar thoughts, and next to them a City Council and State Legislature, and preschool, and…

Chapter Two:

Critical Thinking

Critical thinking: Is clear, reasoned thinking involving critique. Its details vary amongst those who define it. According to *Beyer* (1995), critical thinking means making clear, reasoned judgments. During the process of critical thinking, ideas should be reasoned and well thought out/judged. The National Council for Excellence in Critical Thinking defines critical thinking as the *intellectually disciplined process of actively and skillfully conceptualizing, applying, analyzing, synthesizing, and/or evaluating information gathered from, or generated by, observation, experience, reflection, reasoning, or communication, as a guide to belief and action.*
From Wikipedia

Critical thinking is directly tied to *Political Correctness*. Those who use Political Correctness as a means to manipulate people are quickly exposed when Critical Thinking is employed. Critical Thinking is the light to the cockroach that is Political Correctness.

In this chapter we will explore a few examples of the poison of Political Correctness pulled from our recent history. Although Political Correctness touches almost every aspect of life, it is *race* that has become the poster child for this new PC society.

Before I talk about **racism**, and start misusing the word, which is the new norm, we *should* know what the word *actually* means…

Racism, what is it?

1.
a belief or doctrine that inherent differences among the various human racial groups determine cultural or individual achievement, **usually involving the idea that one's own race is superior** and has the right to dominate others or that a particular racial group is inferior to the others.
2.
a policy, system of government, etc., based upon or fostering such a doctrine; discrimination.
3.
hatred or intolerance of another race or other races.

Dictionary.com

....

1
: a belief that race is the primary determinant of human traits and capacities and that racial differences produce **an inherent superiority of a particular race**
2
: racial prejudice or discrimination

Merriam Webster

....

As its etymology indicates, the first use of the word *racism* is relatively recent—i.e., the 1900s, most literally the 1930s. Linguistically, as the word is a general abstraction that does not in and of itself connote a great deal of positive or negative meaning without additional context (i.e., "racism" = noun of action/condition regarding "race"), its definition and semantics are not entirely settled. Nonetheless, the term is commonly used, often negatively as a pejorative (e.g., "racist"), and is associated with race-based prejudice, violence, dislike, discrimination, or oppression.

Dictionaries define the word as follows:

- The *Oxford English Dictionary* defines racism as the "belief that all members of each race possess characteristics, abilities, or qualities specific to that race, especially so as to distinguish it as **inferior or superior to another race or races**" and the expression of such prejudice.

- *Merriam-Webster's Dictionary* defines it as a belief that race is the primary determinant of human traits and capacities and that racial differences produce **an inherent superiority or inferiority of a particular racial group**, and alternatively that it is also the prejudice based on such a belief.

- The *Macquarie Dictionary* defines racism as: "the belief that human races have distinctive characteristics which determine their respective cultures, usually involving the idea that **one's own race is superior and has the right to rule or dominate others**."

Wikipedia

"...the term is commonly used, often negatively as a pejorative (e.g., "racist"), and is associated with race-based prejudice, violence, dislike, discrimination, or oppression." Wikipedia

That last statement probably sums this up best. The fact is that the 'common use' of the word doesn't really align with its definition, it's being *redefined*. The term *racist*, and *racism*, is used *now* as a general term applied to anyone who says or does something, in the eyes of the person using this term, that demonstrates prejudice (*prejudgment* of someone, in this case based on race) or shows some violence toward someone of another color, or a *dislike* or *disagreement* directed toward someone of another color, or someone who somehow discriminates against or *oppresses* someone who is of a different color. If a black person said, "*Black* lives matter" and you said "*All* lives matter" well, you're a *racist*. If a word is used wrongly by enough people long enough, the 'definition' of the word, at least as far as the general public is concerned, changes. That *has* happened to the word *racist*. I, for example, am certainly NOT racist, according to the dictionary. I don't believe that any race of people is *inherently superior or inferior*. But I do have some negative opinions, and some preconceived notions about some races. Yikes! He sounds like a racist! My opinions are based on *facts*, particularly crime statistics, and *behavior*. Of course none of our opinions, about race in this case, apply to *everyone*, there's always exceptions. But one can, and rightfully, have some opinions, even *general* opinions, that don't necessarily apply to everyone, based on *facts*, and that's OK, and that's not racism.

The following are some examples of media manipulation and exploitation of race in a story:

Note: It's always about *race* if a white person kills, or in some way confronts, or disagrees with, a black person, *always*. You must know that, you've listened to the news from time to time haven't you? But just recently, fresh in the news as of the writing of this book, a black man, a gay black man at that, shot and killed two straight white people, and tried to kill a third, also a white person. But *that* news story, was all about *gun control*. Humm. No mention of a racial angle. **"Black man kills white people"** or **"Gay man kills straight people."** Those were not the headlines. I have no idea for sure if race played any part in that shooting, although some information is coming out that this man *was* obsessed with race, and even wanted to start a race war. But to the media, the story is still all about *gun control*.

Picture the same story with a few changes, *straight white man shoots and kills two gay black people, wounds third gay black person.* Would the headline still be about gun control? That sort of analysis is what *Critical Thinking* is all about. If you don't think, for *yourself* you are a prime target to be *manipulated*. Political Correctness has *changed us*, we think differently, and often non-critically because of it. It has taken decades, but as a society it has worked, we *are* indoctrinated.

Trayvon Martin, it was a big story, and Barack Obama said if he *had a son, he would have looked like Trayvon*. Humm, really? I guess Barack Obama thinks all black people look alike. Do you remember this case? Trayvon Martin was coming home from the store, he had *Skittles* and an "Iced Tea."

Fast forward... George Zimmerman thinks Trayvon is acting suspicious, he calls the police, but before the police arrive Trayvon ends up on top of Zimmerman beating him, and Zimmerman pulls out his gun and shoots Trayvon. Trayvon dies. Witnesses testify that Trayvon was on top of Zimmerman, beating him, and the jury decides Zimmerman was justified in shooting him.

Trayvon was just a *kid* who went to the store to buy some candy and some iced tea. For TV, the media chose a picture of Trayvon several years younger, smiling, not the more *gangsta* looking current photos of Trayvon. Why'd they pick *that* picture? And it wasn't *iced tea*, it was *Arizona Watermelon Fruit Juice Cocktail.* Did you know that Arizona Watermelon Fruit Juice Cocktail, a bag of Skittles, and simple cough syrup make a codeine-based drink called "lean?" Did you hear that on the news? There's an entire online subculture devoted to the use of "lean," which Trayvon was familiar with. There are online posts from Trayvon where he says he could make some "fire-ass lean" using cough syrup, skittles, and Arizona Watermelon Fruit Juice Cocktail. Humm, those were the two items he was heading home with, two-thirds of the ingredients needed to make "lean." Just an innocent smiling kid heading home with Skittles and Iced Tea? He didn't do ANYTHING, the racist Zimmerman just shot him, for no reason. I hate racists.

Trayvon's autopsy showed liver damage in this otherwise healthy young 18-year-old that is consistent with the kind of damage that excessive "lean" usage causes to the liver. Humm. And the psychological symptoms associated with the use of "lean" are extreme *physical aggression* and *paranoia*. Humm. You heard all that on the news, right? There's a reason you didn't hear that on the news, much of the media *manipulates* the news, rather than simply reporting the *facts*. They have an agenda.

Another case… *Michael Brown* in Ferguson, Missouri, it has a huge story; a guy who had just pushed around a store owner, stole a few cigars, and then was 'gunned down' by a racist cop, even though he had his hands up and said, "Don't shoot," remember? Well, except that after stealing those cigars, and pushing around the store owner, he refused to listen to the police officer who told him to get out of the street. Then Michael Brown got into a fight with the officer while the officer sat in his car, trying to take the officer's gun, and then Brown ran away, but turned and charged at the officer, and the officer shot him, and he died. Did you know that the evidence showed he never had his hands up, he *did* try to take the officer's gun, he *did* rush at the officer, "head down like a football player?" I hate racist witnesses, and racist people doing autopsy reports, and… oh, those witnesses were black, and the Obama administration and the black Attorney General did their own autopsy, and did their own investigation of all the facts and THEY also agreed that the police officer was justified in shooting Brown, oh.

Eric Garner on Staten Island, he was just selling illegal cigarettes on the sidewalk when racist cops jumped on him, and he said he couldn't breathe, but they handcuffed him, and he died. They didn't have to do that; he was just selling illegal cigarettes. They didn't need to jump on him and restrain him, just because he wouldn't listen to the police and he resisted getting arrested. *Racists*. They could have just let him sell his cigarettes. Why would the police have to arrest someone committing a crime, and then handcuff somebody resisting arrest, why? Racists, yup, that's why.

Racist cops. Cops hate black people. Black lives *don't* matter. Cops get up in the morning and go out looking for black people to harass or kill. Fucking cops. Racist country. The jails are *full* of black and brown people. Black and brown people are arrested a

LOT more than white people. White people get off, black people go to jail. Have you ever watched an episode of COPS? The racists who make that show fill it up with cops arresting black and brown people, why don't they show more white people getting arrested? Because the cops only go after black and brown people, *racists*. Or, do more black and brown people get arrested because more black and brown people are committing more crime than white people? NO, I'm sure that's just some racist who wants you to believe that!

Does any of that make you think? Maybe it makes you think *differently*? Maybe you begin to see a pattern, a pattern of media and government manipulation? A manipulation of your culture or your race? Humm. *Critical Thinking* is about relying on *facts* not *emotion*. Get a T-Shirt, it says "Hands up don't shoot" or "I can't breathe" or "Black lives matter" because you're making a statement, you're standing up for... uh, you're making a statement about racism? Or you're making another statement, something like *"I'm easily manipulated. I'm not a Critical Thinker."*

It's Politically Correct right now to forget about facts, "Hands up don't shoot."

It's Politically Correct to believe that *racism* is what fills up our prisons with black and brown people, not criminal behavior.

It's Politically Correct to blame the *police* for crime, and for arrests of innocent black or brown people. Innocent? You think? Really? The police just make this stuff up, the people they arrest aren't *really* drug dealers, or thieves, or guilty of some crime? The prisons are full of *innocent* people? You believe that?

This chapter could be a book itself, a *long* one, but this is just a brief discussion of *Critical Thinking*, just a little bit, to make you THINK. We could have used other examples, but *race* is THE most important and *dangerous* example of the poison of Political Correctness. We are being *divided*, for someone's political purpose.

We don't need to ascribe to some wild conspiracy theory, the essence of what's happening is clear. Someone *is* pitting us against each other. For political reasons? To gain power? To control us? Something is going on behind the scenes. We are being manipulated for a *purpose*, someone, some organization, some political party, some agenda is benefiting from growing tension between the races, and growing animosity toward our local police. I like chess, but not when I'm one of the pieces.

<u>Note</u>: *I know there ARE racists, of all colors, and bad cops, and innocent people in jail, etc., duh. Are some cops power-tripping bastards, yes, I've met a couple. Do some lie? Sure, I had one lie to the judge in a traffic ticket case I was involved in. Is there a racial bias among some police officers, sure. But is it systemic? Is it the norm for police officers, no, it isn't. The image you are being sold is manufactured, it doesn't reflect reality or the behavior of most police officers. How do I know this, I'm a Critical Thinker, I've looked at the **facts**.*

You should remain open to a realization that you might have been misled, maybe *intentionally*. Political Correctness is a *political* animal, there are *political* reasons that people and races of people are manipulated, and that reason is *control*. Such 'control' is usually the product of lies; Political Correctness is most often based on a lie. If we realize THAT we can view examples of Political Correctness in a wholly different light. Political Correctness is not 'correct' or how we *should* be acting, as they'd like you to believe. These Politically Correct ideas are a method used to *manipulate*. Manipulating us and dividing us by race is a powerful tool, and those with political ambitions are using that tool, and it's working.

Political power comes from the ability to control people and their opinions. Political Correctness should be viewed skeptically, for what it is, a tool for *control*. Do you like being controlled? I don't. Do you like being manipulated as a pawn for some political agenda? I don't. Let's think first and assemble the facts before we act. Let's break free of the chains of somebody or some party's political agenda. Let's be who we are meant to be, "We the People" *united*, all of us, regardless of color, we are *The People*.

Let's remember that the Federal Government was created *by* the *People* of the *States*. WE granted IT *limited* powers, IT does not control the People, WE control IT. *(At least that's the way it's meant to be, and WE **can** make that happen)* but you have to break free of the control of the political manipulators, and you need to recognize the lies of Political Correctness through the process of Critical Thinking. Our *brains* are all the same color.

Come close, I'll tell you a secret...

This 'secret' is VERY politically incorrect. I'm white (that's not a secret, but this is) Shuuuu, don't tell anyone, but I've spent many decades *infiltrating* white society. I know their secrets. I've been inside the fire departments, *and* the police departments. I've even carried a gun and handcuffs. I took notes. I listened carefully. I had secret meetings with groups of white people. I'll tell you what I learned. We white people, most of us in my opinion, we judge people as 'people' not people of a certain color, but as *people*. It's true, we do, and to *most* of us, in my experience, we white people judge people based on their 'Character' *not* their color.

But... I'll tell you another secret about myself. I *have* dealt with lots of racists. I've seen them at work, on TV, and there are LOTS of them. In my experience these people think about *color* a LOT, they judge people based on color *all the time*. I've seen this from reporters on television, I've seen this from LOTS of politicians, even *Presidents*, and I've seen this from hundreds of protestors, their overwhelming *obsession* with **color**. These racists I've discovered, are mostly *black* and increasingly *brown*. I've looked for white ones, but I just haven't found them. During my police training I was waiting for the secret handshake, for the meeting of white officers who would tell me all about the secret police agenda, of going out each day to harass and/or kill black people, but, that meeting never happened. The racists I've observed are virtually ALL black. That's just me, I'm sure some other white infiltrators have discovered some white racists, I'm *sure* of it, but I didn't. I don't think there are a lot of them; I was *looking* for them, but I couldn't find them. Now keep that secret quiet because it's NOT Politically Correct, it flies in the face of EVERYTHING you're being told. Shuuuuuu...

Remember the *poison* of Political Correctness? That poison is the poison of **lies**, it is the agenda of *control* that is at the heart of Political Correctness.

And so, the message here, of *The Poison of Political Correctness*, is simple really. You *will* be bombarded with sound bites that mislead. You will face a media who hope you *don't* think it out, who want you to react with *emotion* not facts; they want to *lead* you. They want to *direct* you. They want you to think and to *vote* based on misplaced emotion, lies, and slogans; without investigating the facts.

For those of you in school, you'll often face an educational monopoly that thrives in that world, a world that hopes you *won't* utilize critical thinking unless that thinking adopts *their* facts, and *their* agenda. When you stop, and look, and take the time to investigate the *other side* of the issue you'll often discover that the call for *diversity* and *tolerance* has no place for diverse views, and is *only* tolerant of those who adopt the party line.

Abortion, global warming, capitalism, war, oil, corporations, immigration, LGBTQ issues, religion, marriage... forming opinions on such issues requires inquiry, not a quick scan of *Facebook* or *Twitter* or *Instagram* posts, or the opinion of some particular talking head on the news, or the views of the host of some TV comedy "news" show.

Critical Thinking is *required* of the voter. *You* will shape the future and that future should be based on *facts* and information, not some T-Shirt slogan or some politician's idea of what's good for you.

Political Correctness wants you to *follow* not lead. It embraces the *emotion* of those who would shout down and silence the speaker. Those who are out to sell the notion of Political Correctness would rather you didn't *think*, just *listen*, to *them*. **THEY** know what you *should* think.

My little court case, the one that began this book, it's a good example of a mind-set. Those supposed "educators" didn't want my students to hear a view, or words, that *they* didn't like. For all their touting of **Critical Thinking** *they* wanted to *control* thought and opinion. They didn't want another viewpoint to compete. They were willing to disregard our most essential Constitutional and human right, that of free speech and free thought.

Those people, that institutional bureaucracy, has an agenda, one that had been poisoned over time by *Political Correctness*. Those people and millions like them have been indoctrinated, often willingly, with this poison. *Truth,* and *Freedom*, and *speech*… that is the cure.

We are not our colors, we are what's inside.

-Lance Hodge

Note: If you're one of my EMT students, be prepared to discuss these issues. I'm prepared for you to disagree, and to support your side of the discussion with *facts*, not just emotion.

BE CAREFUL,
WORDS ARE DANGEROUS,
WORDS CAUSE THOUGHT!

DO NOT THINK!*

DANGER:

*MAKE SURE YOU *SPEAK* AND *HEAR*
ONLY *APPROVED* WORDS!

*The above warning has been a public service of *Political Correctness*

Summary for the EMT

Race, Religion, Sex, Politics, and Culture, are all important factors to keep in mind as we deal with each other and with the public, and we should be mindful and respectful of the beliefs of others, even when we disagree.

Our goal should be that of always giving the highest level of patient care to *every* person we encounter. We should strive to treat *every* person with the same compassion and care as we would give a loved one.

Diversity of opinion must seek, when possible, tolerance of views we do not agree with; but tolerance does not mean we must ultimately *share* those views to prove our commitment to diversity.

We should embrace our *individuality* of opinion and need not *embrace* the ideas of another.

Think for yourself!

Statistics regarding crime and race:

2008 (Jan-June) <u>New York City Crime Statistics by Race</u>

(From Yahoo News)

-83% of all gun *assailants* were black, while making up 24% of the population

-Blacks and Hispanics together accounted for 98% of all gun assailants

-49 of every 50 muggings and murders were carried out by blacks or Hispanics

-Blacks and Hispanics commit 96% of the crimes in New York
http://americanfreepress.net/?p=14864

Nearly 50% of all black males and 38% of white men will be arrested by the age of 23. These statistics, compiled by four college professors between the years 1997-2008, were published in the January 6 edition of the journal Crime & Delinquency.

A 2012 study by the Department of Justice's Office of Juvenile Justice and Delinquency Prevention revealed that in 2010 **black youths committed six times more murders, three times more rapes, 10 times more robberies and three times more assaults than did their white counterparts**. Similar statistics were released by the Federal Bureau of Investigation (FBI) in the "Uniform Crime Reports." They determined, "In the year 2008, **black youths, who make up 16% of the youth population, accounted for 52% of juvenile violent crime arrests, including**

58% for homicide and 67% for robbery." By contrast, the only categories where white youths surpassed blacks were in liquor law violations and driving under the influence.

Even black civil rights advocates such as Van Jones, President Barack Obama's former green jobs czar, confirmed these findings. In his October 5, 2005 article, "Are Blacks a Criminal Race?" Jones wrote, **"African American youth represent 32% of all weapons arrests [and] were arrested for aggravated assault at a rate nearly three times that of whites." –**

http://americanfreepress.net/?p=14864#sthash.2hSbocuW.dpuf

Similar statistics abound. *Google* this stuff. Take care that the 'facts' you find don't always come from those with a political agenda; such 'facts' are often lies dressed up as facts.

You know that most media outlets have political agendas, right? *Listen* to opposing views, opposing news shows, opposing political parties, to friends you agree with and to friends you *don't* agree with, and THINK about what you hear.

When you begin to recognize an *agenda,* you'll often recognize the intent to *control* your thinking, and the lies should begin to stand out; you'll begin to see behind the curtain. You may find yourself thinking twice before 'liking' the link you've just been sent; a *thinker* stops to think.

You, all of us, are a chess piece to those who seek power; you'll hear the truth and you'll hear the lies if you listen to both sides of an issue. Can you recognize the truth, the lies? *They* hope you can't.

Here it comes; peer pressure, powerful agenda driven media manipulators at work, social networks with a social/political agenda, all trying to control how and what you think… but you'll figure that out, you're a *Critical Thinker*, right?

Other books by Lance Hodge

Available at **Amazon.com**, Booksamillion.com, Barnes & Noble, and other fine book sellers.

Made in the USA
Coppell, TX
23 July 2023

19507261R00036